Up

by Tameron Dennis
illustrated by Eva Vagreti

Core Decodable 2

McGraw Hill Education

Bothell, WA • Chicago, IL • Columbus, OH • New York, NY

MHEonline.com

Send all inquiries to:
McGraw-Hill Education
8787 Orion Place
Columbus, OH 43240

ISBN: 978-0-02-145133-3
MHID: 0-02-145133-8

Printed in Canada.

9 10 11 12 KOD 24

Is the  up?

sun

The  is up.

sun

Is the  up?

boy

See the  ?

clock

See the  !

clock

The  is up!

boy